Other DILBERT® books from Andrews McMeel Publishing

For ordering information, call 1-800-223-2336.

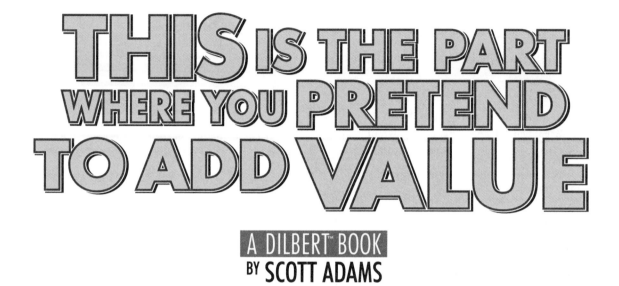

THIS IS THE PART WHERE YOU PRETEND TO ADD VALUE

A DILBERT™ BOOK
BY SCOTT ADAMS

08 09 10 11 12 RR2 10 9 8 7 6 5 4 3 2 1

ISBN-13: 978-0-7407-7227-6
ISBN-10: 0-7407-7227-9

Library of Congress Control Number: 2007937790

www.andrewsmcmeel.com
www.dilbert.com

For Shelly

Introduction

If I had to describe my sixteen years of corporate work with one phrase, it would be "pretending to add value." At the risk of bragging, I did it well. Given that you are reading a *Dilbert* book right now, you too are probably skilled at bluffing your way to a paycheck. I respect that.

You might have noticed that corporations hum along no matter who is sick, vacationing, or recently dead. Any one person's value on any particular day is vanishingly small. The key to career advancement is appearing valuable despite all hard evidence to the contrary. If you pretend well enough, you can become CEO. At that point, the gap between actual and perceived value is enormous. That causes a form of stress that can only be eased via a process involving unreasonably high compensation, boats, and trophy spouses.

If you add any *actual* value to your company today, your career is probably not moving in the right direction. Real work is for people at the bottom who plan to stay there. Luckily, you can get your illusion of value back on track by reading this book at work and claiming you are looking for "good ones" to put in your PowerPoint presentation. No one will ask if your presentation is necessary, or if you have a presentation to give. All that will matter is that you appear to be adding value. And if innocent people get hurt in the process, that's called leadership.

Speaking of leadership, there is still time to join Dogbert's New Ruling Class and rule by his side when he conquers the world. Just sign up for the free *Dilbert* newsletter that is published approximately whenever I feel like it. To sign up, go to www.dilbert.com and follow the subscription instructions. If that doesn't work for some reason, send an e-mail to newsletter@unitedmedia.com.

S. Adams

Scott Adams

21

YOU MIGHT HEAR SOME NOISE FROM THE BASEMENT TONIGHT.

I GOT A BIG ORDER FOR RUNNING SHOES, SO I'M MAKING THE ELBONIANS WORK AROUND THE CLOCK.

HERE'S SOME PEPPER SPRAY IN CASE ANY OF THEM ESCAPE.

PLEASE HELP ME. YOUR DOG HAS ENSLAVED MY PEOPLE IN YOUR BASE-MENT AND FORCED US TO MAKE RUNNING SHOES!

GAAA!!! MY EYES!!!

PSSST

I LIKE TO HELP PEOPLE, BUT I ALSO LIKE INEXPENSIVE FOOTWEAR.

WE HAVE A REPORT OF A CARTOONIST IN CUBICLE 4S950. HIS COMICS MIGHT EMBARRASS THE COMPANY.

WE CAN'T FIRE HIM BECAUSE IT WOULD LOOK BAD. YOU MUST GIVE HIM ABSURD ASSIGNMENTS UNTIL HE QUITS.

YOUR NEW JOB IS TO EVALUATE TECHNOLOGY THAT OBVIOUSLY HAS NO ECONOMICAL APPLICATION.

WOO HOO!

30

33

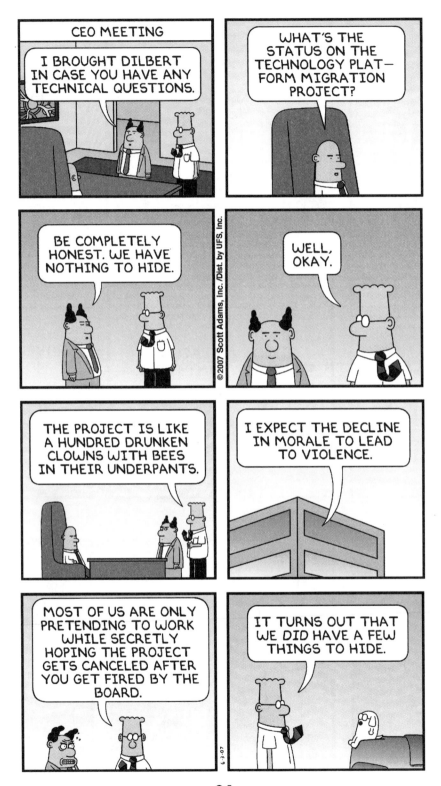

39

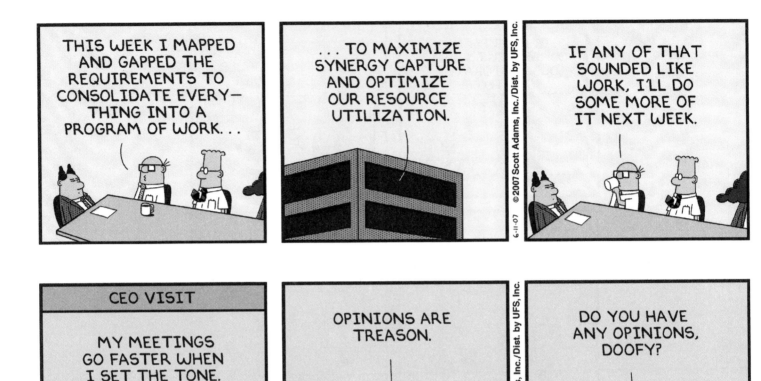

40

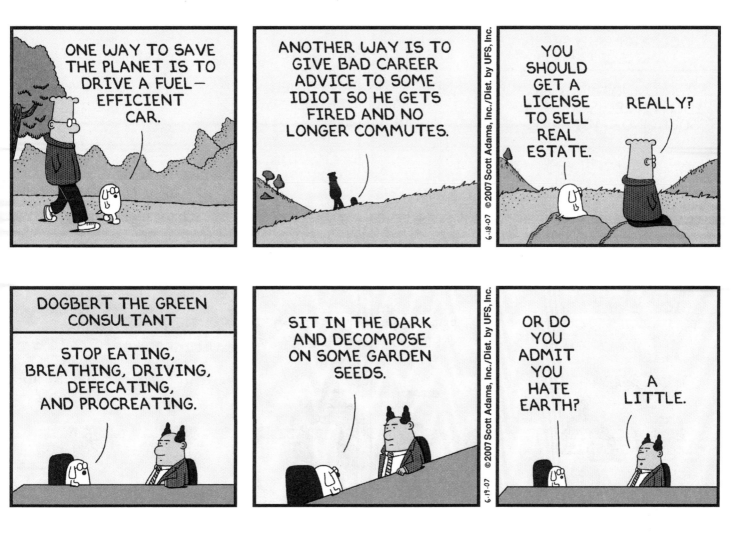

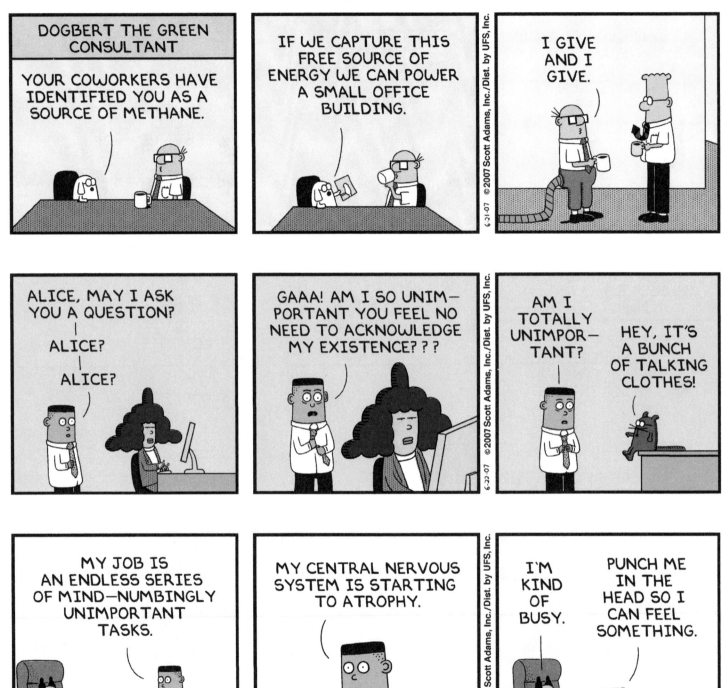

47

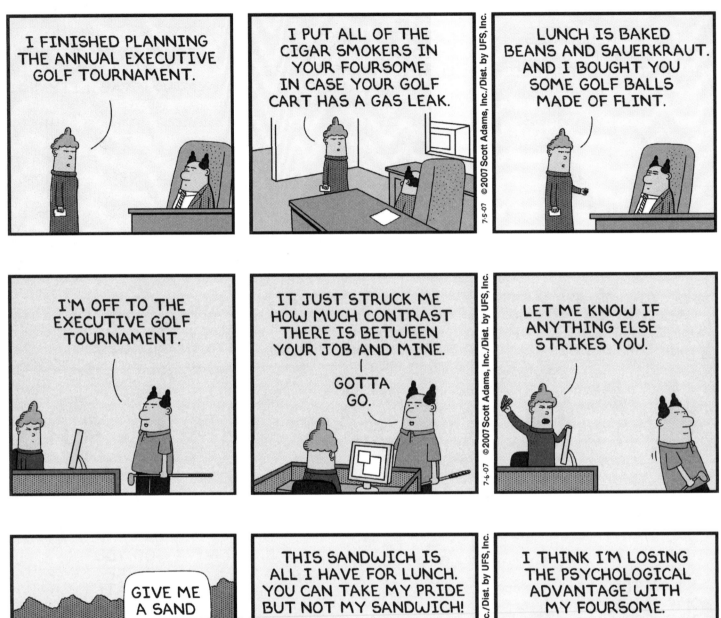

54

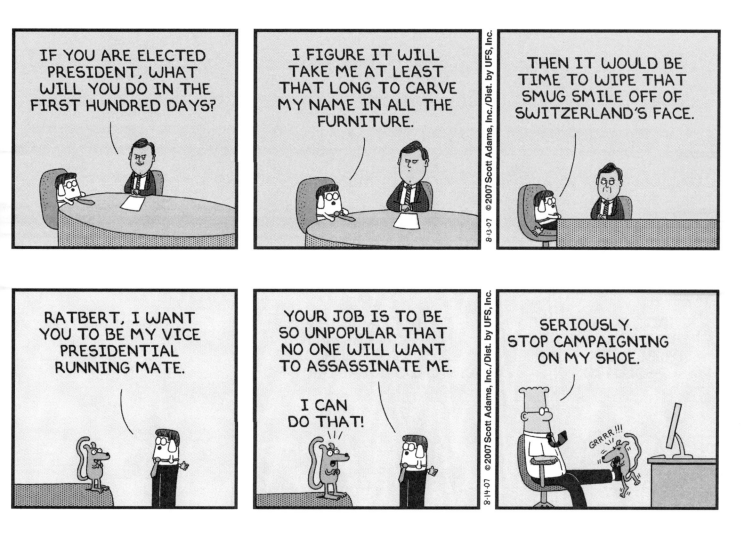

69

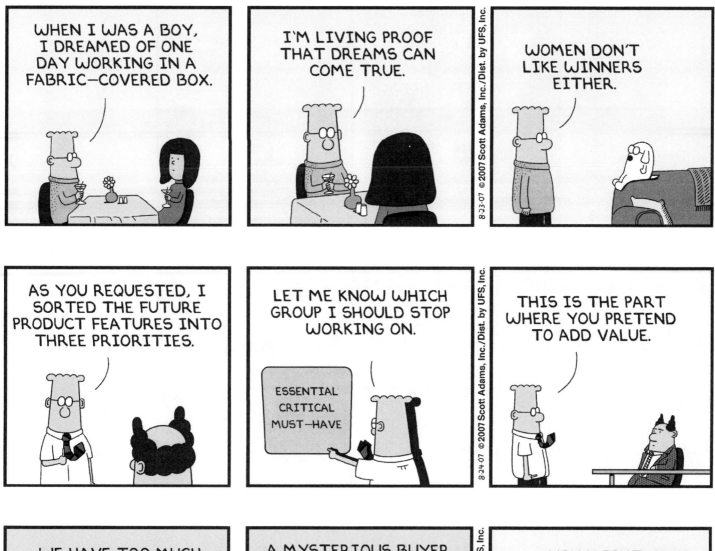

71

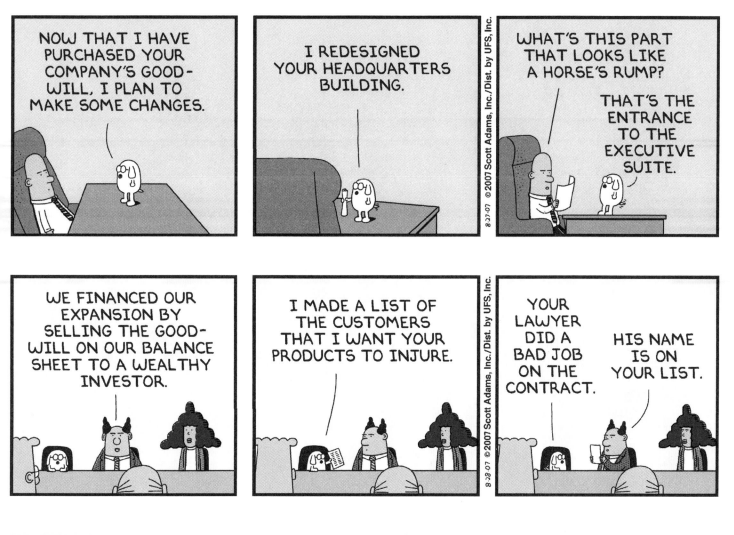

75

79

WE CAN'T COMPETE ON PRICE.

WE ALSO CAN'T COMPETE ON QUALITY, FEATURES OR SERVICE.

THAT LEAVES FRAUD, WHICH I'D LIKE YOU TO CALL MARKETING.

OUR NEW VP OF MARKETING PROMISES TO IMPROVE OUR REVENUES BY TEN BILLION PERCENT!

THAT IS A RIDICULOUS LIE THAT ONLY A GULLIBLE MORON WOULD BELIEVE.

OH YEAH? HOW DO YOU EXPLAIN THE FACT THAT *HE* BELIEVED IT?

TOUCHÉ

DOGBERT, THE VP OF MARKETING

IT'S MY JOB TO SPRAYPAINT THE ROADKILL.

I'LL USE A PROCESS THE EXPERTS CALL "DISHONESTY."

MY MOTTO IS "IF IT ISN'T IMMORAL, IT PROBABLY WON'T WORK."

91

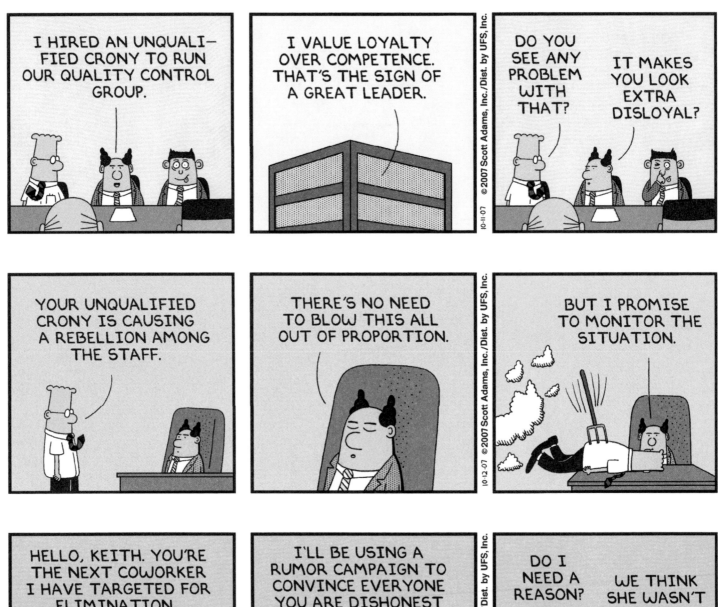

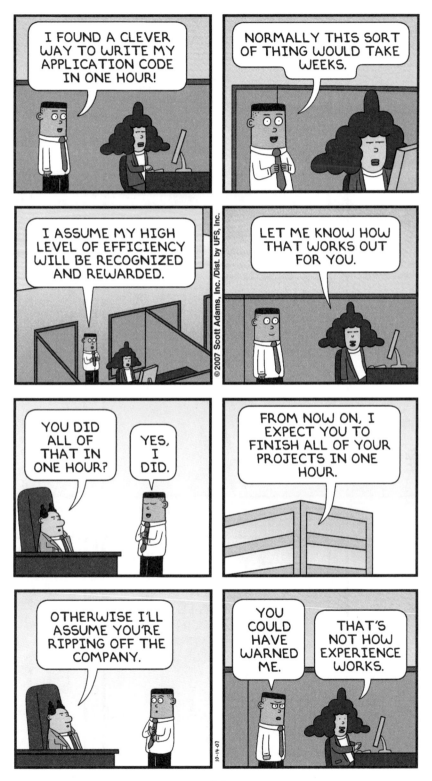

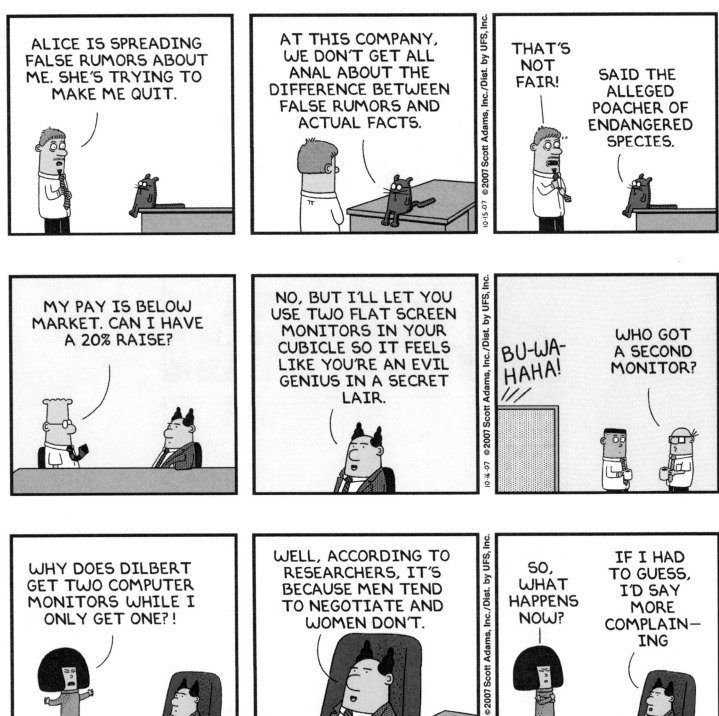

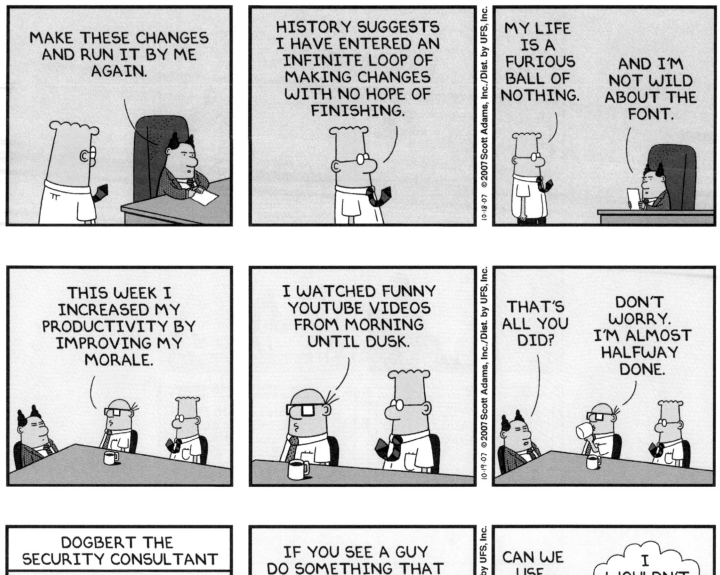

99

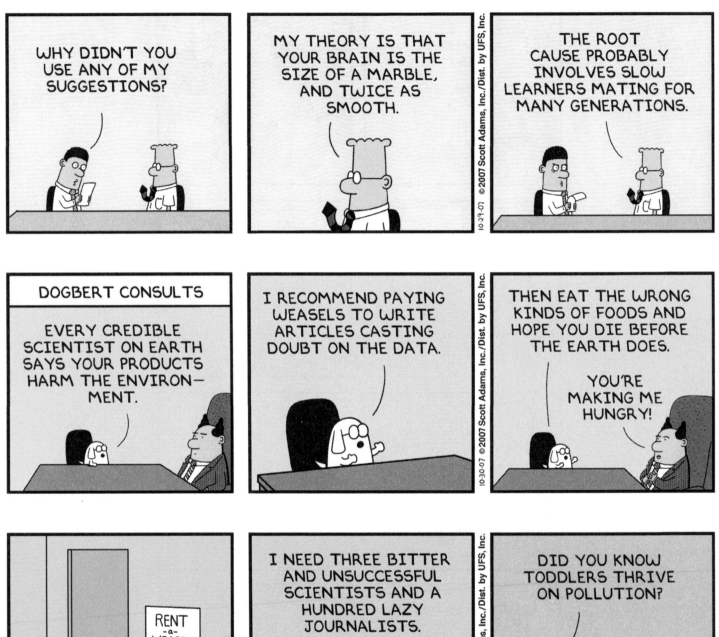

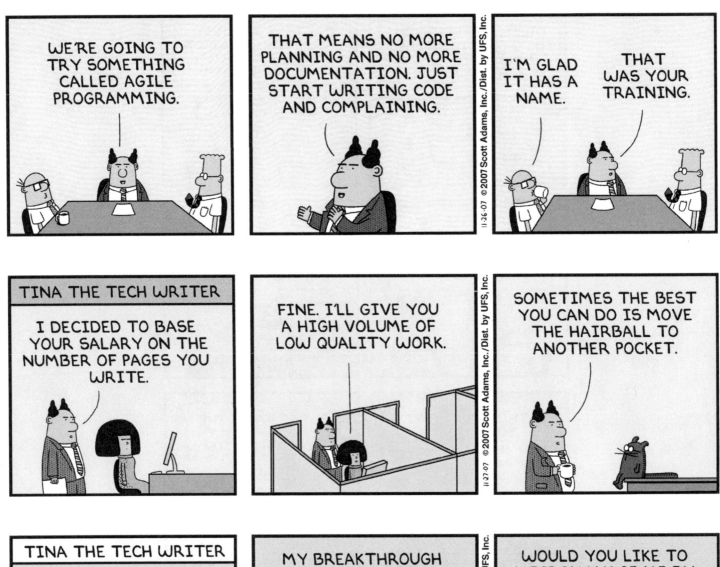

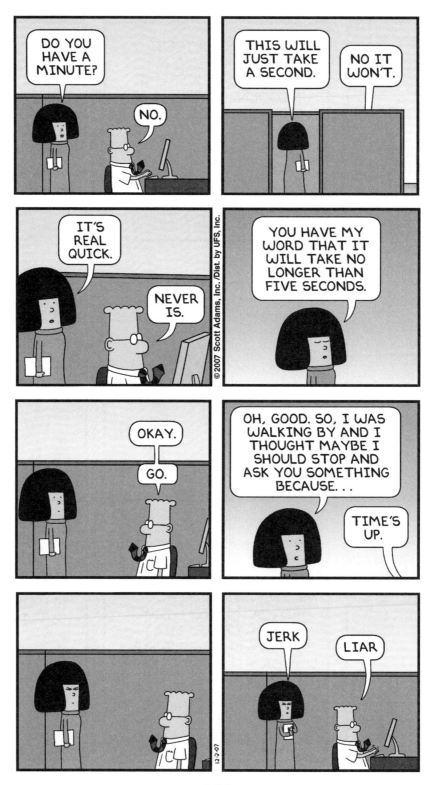

DON'T WORRY, ASOK. THE PROTOTYPE IS PERFECTLY SAFE.

I FOUND YOU A CO-PILOT. HE'S A BIT GRIM, BUT HE WORKS FOR FREE.

HEY, I WONDER WHAT THIS BUTTON DOES.

I AM SAD TO REPORT THAT ASOK THE INTERN DIED DURING A TEST OF OUR MOON SHUTTLE PROTOTYPE.

BEFORE HE LEFT, HE PUT A SAMPLE OF HIS DNA IN A JAR. HIS PLAN IS TO REINCARNATE INTO HIS OWN CLONE.

WHERE'S THE JAR WITH ASOK'S DNA?

I NEEDED A SECOND CANDY JAR.

YOUR PROTOTYPE KILLED ASOK. THAT MEANS IT IS YOUR JOB TO CLONE HIM AND HOPE HE REINCARNATES INTO THE CLONE.

CAROL USED HIS DNA CONTAINER FOR A SNACK JAR, SO BE CAREFUL.

WHY DO I FEEL NUTS?

YOU'RE PART SNICKERS BAR.

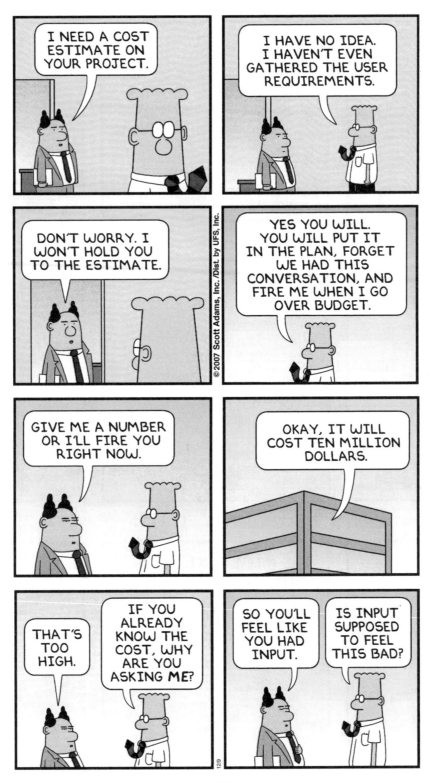

YOU HAVE GOOD EXPERIENCE AS A DEAD HORSE, BUT CAN YOU TAKE A BEATING?

SO, YOU THINK YOU CAN IGNORE MY QUESTIONS, DO YOU?

CANCEL ALL OF MY MEETINGS. THIS COULD TAKE A FEW MORE HOURS.

I HIRED A DEAD HORSE. HE DOESN'T LOOK LIKE MUCH, BUT IF YOU BEAT HIM LONG ENOUGH, HE DOES GOOD WORK.

HAVE YOU SEEN HIM DO GOOD WORK?

I HAVEN'T BEATEN HIM LONG ENOUGH.

INTRODUCE YOURSELF TO THE OTHERS!

WHAP!

I'M NOT ALLOWED TO DISCUSS THE COMPANY POLITICS THAT FORM A CAREER MINEFIELD AROUND YOUR PROJECT.

AND I CAN'T TELL YOU THE COMPANY'S NEW STRATEGIC DIRECTION, OR ANYTHING ABOUT OUR UPCOMING REORG.

MY PLAN IS TO CRITICIZE YOU UNTIL SOMETHING GOOD HAPPENS.

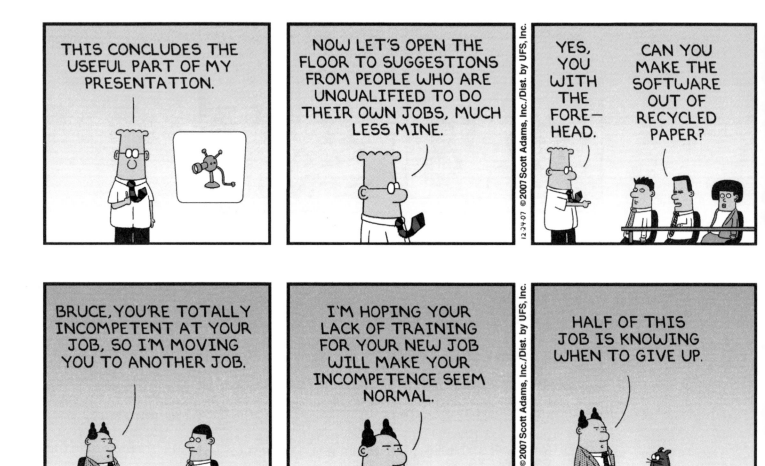